W9-AKW-624

Going Green

Traveling Green

by Jacqueline A. Ball

Consultant: Adrienne Greve, Ph.D.
Assistant Professor, City and Regional Planning Department
California Polytechnic State University, San Luis Obispo, California

BEARPORT

Credits

Cover and Title Page, © age fotostock/SuperStock; 5, © Arne Trautmann/iStockphoto; 6-7, © Ted Aljibe/AFP/
Getty Images; 7, © Brian Snyder/Reuters/Landov; 8-9, © Robert Sorbo/Reuters/Landov; 10T, © Imaginechina
via AP Images; 10M, © G. Bowater/Corbis; 10B, © Peter Horree/Alamy; 11, © AP Images/Angela Rowlings; 12, ©
Peter Scholey/Alamy; 13, © Armin Weigel/dpa/Landov; 14, © Paul Hill/Alamy; 15, © Steve Parsons/PA Photos/
Landov; 16-17, © Mitchell Funk/Photographer's Choice/Getty Images; 18-19, © Tim Post/Minnesota Public Radio;
20, © Reuters/Landov; 21, © Mario Tama/Getty Images; 23, © John Cogill/Bloomberg News/Landov; 24, ©
Marcelo Rudini/Alamy; 25, © PTT Medical/Newscom; 26, © Ryan McGinnis/Alamy; 27, © Jeffrey Blackler/Alamy;
28L, © Image Source Pink/Alamy; 28R, © Oramstock/Alamy; 29, © Jim Wright/Star Ledger/Corbis; 30, © Jaren
Jai Wicklund/Shutterstock.

Publisher: Kenn Goin
Senior Editor: Lisa Wiseman
Creative Director: Spencer Brinker
Photo Researcher: Lindsay Blatt

The Going Green series is
printed on recycled paper.

Library of Congress Cataloging-in-Publication Data

Ball, Jacqueline A.
  Traveling green / by Jacqueline A. Ball.
     p. cm. — (Going green)
  Includes bibliographical references and index.
  ISBN-13: 978-1-59716-964-6 (library binding : alk. paper)
  ISBN-10: 1-59716-964-1 (library binding : alk. paper)
  1. Travel—Environmental aspects—Juvenile literature. 2. Transportation—Environmental aspects—Juvenile literature. I. Title.
  G156.5.E58B33 2010
  790.1'8—dc22
                              2009019836

For more information, write to Bearport Publishing Company, Inc., 101 Fifth Avenue, Suite 6R, New York, New York 10003.
Printed in the United States of America.

10 9 8 7 6 5 4 3 2 1

Contents

Ready, Set—Go Green!

In today's world, people are always on the go. Whether a trip covers a thousand miles (km) or a few blocks, it requires **energy**. Not all energy is the same, though. The kind of energy that comes from the sun or wind, for example, is **renewable**—it will never run out. The kind of energy that powers most cars, however, is **nonrenewable**. It comes from **fossil fuels** such as oil and gas. Once people use up Earth's supply of these fuels, they can't be replaced. Burning these fuels also pollutes the air and releases harmful **greenhouse gases**, such as **carbon dioxide**, that contribute to **global warming**. If Earth's climate warms up too quickly, the homes of some kinds of plants and animals could be damaged or destroyed.

To protect the planet and preserve energy resources, people need to use more **sustainable** methods of travel—transportation that is less wasteful, cleaner, and depends more on renewable energy. In other words, people need to travel **green**.

Greenest to Least Green Methods of Travel
Walking, Biking, Skateboarding
Mass Transit (buses, subways, trains)
Carpooling
Airplanes; cars carrying only one passenger

Traveling by means that don't involve engines, such as walking, hiking, biking, and skating, are the greenest ways to go short distances. They are also the healthiest!

Quick and Dirty

More than four billion people travel by air every year. Planes are the fastest type of transportation, but they're also the worst for the environment. Flying pumps out more pounds (kg) of carbon dioxide per person than almost any other form of travel. Air travel also releases more greenhouse gases higher up in the atmosphere than other forms of travel, which scientists believe speeds up global warming faster than pollution on the ground.

In the United States, two-thirds of all oil that's used goes toward powering vehicles.

Experts say people should travel by train or bus instead of by air whenever possible. Trains are four to ten times less polluting than planes, mostly because they require much less power to move. Buses are also a greener way to travel than planes, with better engine technology and new fuels making them cleaner all the time.

Airports around the world, such as this one in Boston, Massachusetts, are usually full of travelers.

Leaner and Greener

Airplanes may be a lot greener in the future. The airlines are making big changes in planes, starting with their weight. Why does weight matter? As a plane flies, it has to push through the air. The faster it goes and the heavier it is, the harder it has to push. Lots of jet fuel is burned to overcome air resistance, which is the force of the air that pushes back against the plane as it moves forward.

Manufacturers are now using **composite materials** instead of heavy aluminum and steel to build new airplanes. These materials are made up of such substances as plastic foam and tough **carbon fibers**, which are strong yet lightweight. Building lighter airplanes will make it easier for them to overcome air resistance. It will also help them use less fossil fuels in flight.

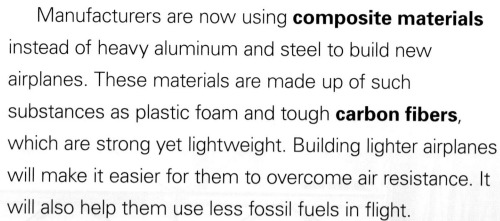

Boeing's 787 Dreamliner, which was built using some composite materials, uses almost 30 percent less fuel than other airplanes.

The Dreamliner

The Need for Speed

Since flying is bad for the environment, people going on trips, especially short ones, should find other ways to travel. For example, high-speed trains, which run on electricity, create fewer greenhouse gases than airplanes.

A Maglev train in China

Many high-speed trains are now in use around the world. One of the quickest is the Maglev train in Shanghai, China. Its top speed is about 259 miles per hour (417 kph). The TGV train in France and the bullet trains in Japan are also fast. They can go up to about 200 miles per hour (322 kph). New high-speed trains are being planned that will travel even faster.

A TGV train in France

Currently, America's only high-speed train is the Acela, which runs between Boston and Washington, D.C., in the northeastern United States. However, California is working on a high-speed train that will run between San Francisco and Los Angeles.

A bullet train in Japan

In the Midwest, officials say high-speed trains connecting Chicago with major cities in nine states could be operating by 2013 or 2014.

Amtrak's Acela picking up passengers at South Station in Boston, Massachusetts

Plugged In

Cars are less harmful to the environment than airplanes, but they are still damaging. Most of the one billion vehicles on the road today have **internal combustion engines**, which burn fossil fuels that release greenhouse gases. To help people travel green, manufacturers are creating vehicles that use less of these fuels. For example, plug-in hybrid cars, trucks, and buses have both a gasoline engine and an electric motor. The motor has a battery that can be recharged by plugging it into an electric socket. The electric motor provides extra power so the engine doesn't use as much gas climbing hills and traveling at high speeds.

There are also many other types of vehicles that are considered green. **Fuel-cell**-powered cars, trucks, and buses use a device that converts **hydrogen** and **oxygen**, which are renewable fuels, into electricity. Plug-in electric cars, bikes, and scooters run on rechargeable batteries that produce zero **emissions**. While plug-ins are good for the environment, most can travel only at low speeds and need to be recharged often.

These soldiers are driving an electric car around an army base in Germany.

Vehicles that are powered only by electricity don't directly emit greenhouse gases. However, if the electricity they use comes from a power plant that burns fossil fuels, then they're indirectly causing pollution. Power plants that produce electricity from solar or wind power do not cause air pollution. Nuclear power plants also do not produce greenhouse gases, but they create other kinds of environmental pollution.

Gas from the Garden

What if people could grow new fuels to "feed" their cars the same way they grow vegetables to feed themselves? In fact, they can! Some fuels today, called **biofuels**, are made from plant materials. One of the benefits of biofuels is that they are renewable—plants grow back so that they can always be used as a source of energy. In addition, plants absorb carbon dioxide as they grow, so the air pollution created by burning plant-based fuels is partly canceled out.

Ethanol is a biofuel made from corn, sugarcane, and other crops. About 12 percent of automobile fuel sold today contains ethanol mixed with gasoline. Some new vehicles are designed to run entirely on pure ethanol or unleaded gas. They are called **flex-fuel vehicles**.

One problem with ethanol, however, is that it uses crops people need for food. That's why some scientists are excited about algae as an ethanol source. Algae, a plantlike organism that grows in water, is available everywhere—and people don't eat it!

A corn crop

Ethanol isn't just for cars. In 2008, a Virgin Atlantic Airways plane flew from London to Amsterdam on a blend of regular fuel and ethanol made from coconut and palm tree oils. Other airlines are trying biofuels, too.

This is the Virgin Atlantic flight that flew using a blend of regular fuel and ethanol. It was the first biofuel flight made by an airline.

City Travel

In U.S. cities, people use a car for 90 percent of their trips. Unfortunately, driving pollutes the air and wastes fuel when cars are stuck in traffic jams. However, there are many ways to travel green in a city. For example, ride a bike. Many cities now offer dedicated bike lanes, no-car zones, and other things to make biking easier. Visitors to Paris, France, can borrow a bike through a city-run program at no charge. In San Francisco, California, visitors can park their bikes in garages just like cars. This gives them a safe and convenient place to leave their bikes while they tour the city.

Another way to travel green is to use public transportation. Riding on buses and subways produces about half as much carbon dioxide per person as riding in private vehicles. These forms of mass transit also move many people at once, keeping cars off the road. Of course, one of the easiest methods of green travel is walking. Not only is it sustainable, but it's good for a person's health.

Many people in New York City choose to walk to work.

Compared to a person riding alone in a car, a bus carrying 40 passengers requires one-sixth of the energy per person to operate. At the same time, it replaces six city blocks' worth of cars.

French-Fried Ride

Most buses, including those used in cities, have **diesel engines**, which emit more pounds of carbon dioxide per mile (km) than gas-powered ones. New diesel fuels, like **biodiesel**, are changing that.

Biodiesel fuels are made from plant products or animal fats. This idea isn't new. In the early 1900s, many of the first diesel engines ran on peanut oil. Today, riders in St. Cloud, Minnesota, can hop on a bus partially powered by used French fry oil. The oil has been recycled from a local college's food service provider and blended with regular diesel fuel.

The Husky Fried Ride is the name of the bus in St. Cloud, Minnesota, that runs on used French fry oil.

reduces reliance on diesel fuel · recycles locally used vegetable oil · reduces emissions Husky Fried Ride

RECYCLE & REUSE.

HuskyFriedRide
fueled with recycl...

Even though biodiesel is made from renewable sources, there are some disadvantages to using it. For example, it can cause an increase in some harmful pollutants, it can decrease the power of an engine, and it is not always readily available.

Heavy Duty

Many cities stay green by relying on a heavy rail system, which is an electric subway or elevated train system that can carry lots of people. Heavy rail systems run on tracks under the streets or on trestles above the streets, bypassing traffic to give riders a fast, smooth ride.

In New York City, officials estimate that 400 million pounds (181 million kg) of pollutants are kept out of the air each year because 1.6 billion people ride the subway instead of driving. It's easy for people in New York City to take the subway. Most live or work near a subway station. This high **population density** makes the subway convenient to use and easy to manage. Cities where homes and offices are farther apart would need more stations and more tracks for the same convenience.

Conveniently located subway stations make it easy for New Yorkers to take the subway.

Commuters inside a crowded subway car

Due to mass transit, New Yorkers use one-quarter as much energy per person, on average, as most people in America.

Green Light for Light Rail

Another way that cities try to encourage green travel is with light rail systems, which carry people short distances. The vehicles that make up a light rail system travel on tracks that are usually at street level, and they are powered by electricity. One advantage of light rail systems is that they can travel slowly through crowded city centers, but rapidly reach highway speeds when they're away from crowds.

However, the best trains, cars, or buses in the world won't do much good if no one uses them! Experts agree that the key to the planet's future lies in green travel. People must change their habits so that walking, biking, and using mass transit become as routine as hopping into a car is now.

In the United States, 855 million gallons (3 billion l) of gasoline are saved by people taking mass transit—the same amount of energy needed to power one-fourth of all U.S. homes in a year. Still, public transportation accounts for only 2 percent of the total trips taken.

Light rail service in
Dublin, Ireland

Case Study #1:
Curitiba, Brazil

In the 1960s, when city planners in Curitiba, Brazil, noticed how fast the population was growing, they were worried. It wasn't that they didn't welcome the newcomers. They just didn't want their beautiful, historic town turned into a polluted parking lot by thousands of additional cars.

To solve this problem, they decided to create a bus system that was so good that people would want to use it instead of driving. They set aside two-way lanes on the city's five major roads for buses only. Then they expanded the bus routes and linked them up so people could easily travel anyplace in the city. Car traffic decreased so much that several streets were no longer needed for cars and were replaced with malls and shopping centers. Pollution levels began to drop, too. Today, two-thirds of all trips through Curitiba are by bus, even though many people own a car.

Buses in Curitiba, Brazil

Case Study #2: Portland, Oregon

About the same time Curitiba was starting to plan for all the new people coming into town, Portland, Oregon, was watching businesses and residents move out to the suburbs. Today, downtown Portland is thriving, however.

What happened? Portland built a mass transit system that brought everything—and everybody—together. The system uses buses and light-rail trains that link suburbs to the city and also to one another.

Portland also created 260 miles (418 km) of bike trails and lanes, including one that goes to the airport. Today, Portland is known as the top cycling city in America. Families ride bikes along the river or down wide streets where no cars are allowed. Eight times as many Portland residents bike to work as in the rest of the country. The city even runs a special program that supplies bikes with lights, as well as biking helmets and locks, to low-income adults so they can travel safely to their jobs.

Commuters biking along the Willamette River in Portland, Oregon

Case Study #3:
New York City

For New York City's mass transit system, being green goes beyond buses and trains to the stations where people wait. Small efforts can add up to big green savings.

For instance, the New York subway system now has 22 escalators that slow down and go into "sleep" mode when nobody's using them. When a customer approaches, a sensor tells the escalator to wake up and gradually increase its speed. Each escalator can save lots of power each day.

New **fluorescent lighting** in tunnels and stations is also helping to make the subways greener. The fluorescent bulbs use four to six times less energy than the ones they replaced. They also last ten times longer.

Escalators make it easy for New Yorkers to get down to the subway and back up to street level. However, these machines use a lot of energy.

Reducing Emissions

Most gasoline engines pump 20 pounds (9 kg) of carbon dioxide into the air for every gallon of gas burned. Here are some simple things drivers can do to reduce those emissions. Pass them on to the drivers at your house!

Action	Amount of Carbon Dioxide Kept Out of the Air (pounds per year/kilograms per year)
Travel 600 miles (966 km) by train instead of alone in your car	240/109
Check tires monthly and keep them properly inflated—fully inflated tires help a car get better gas mileage	250/113
Check the car's air filter monthly and replace it when necessary	800/363
Drive 25 fewer miles (40 km) per week	1,500/680
Ride in a carpool with two or more people, two days a week	1,590/721

(Source: StopGlobalWarming.org)

The Toyota Prius hybrid is considered to be one of the most fuel-efficient cars sold in the United States.

Bikes Are Better and Better

Bicycling is great for your health and for the environment, but most bikes are too heavy and awkward to carry onto a crowded subway or bus. To solve this problem, manufacturers are making bikes that are lighter. A bike with a bamboo frame instead of a metal one is light enough to carry and is made from materials that are renewable. The frames of the bikes are even crash resistant.

Other manufacturers are producing portable bikes. They fold in half for easy storage. This makes it easier for more people to use bikes as part of their daily commute.

A portable bike

It's easy to lock up and store a bike that folds. It doesn't take up much room.

Shrink Your Footprint

Want a quick look at the impact you're making on Earth? Answer these five questions. The more "yes" answers, the larger your carbon footprint, which is the amount of greenhouse gases produced by one person's activities, is likely to be.

1. Have you traveled by plane in the past year?

2. Do you ride in a car more than two times a week?

3. Do you walk to school or to after-school activities fewer than two times a week?

4. Do you ride your bike to school or to after-school activities fewer than two times a week?

5. Does your family buy food that has been shipped long distances in order to get to your supermarket?

Want to calculate your exact carbon footprint? Go to:

globalwarming.house.gov/getinvolved?id=0005

Walking is one of the greenest ways to get to school.

Cutting down on driving by only a few miles (km) a day can keep tons of carbon dioxide out of the air. These things can help your family cut down on car time:

- Tell the drivers in your family that you'd rather walk or ride your bike whenever safety and weather allow.

- Start a "walk to school" or "bike to school" week with the kids in your neighborhood.

- Help the adults in your family limit car trips to the grocery store by suggesting they buy more food during each trip.

- Suggest that your family buy products grown or made locally. You'll support your community and reduce the emissions caused by transporting products long distances.

- When you take a trip, pack only what you need. The lighter the load, the less fuel your car will burn.

Learn More Online

To learn more about traveling green, visit
www.bearportpublishing.com/GoingGreen

Glossary

biodiesel (*bye*-oh-DEE-zuhl) a type of fuel made from living animal or plant matter for use in diesel engines

biofuels (BY-oh-*fyoo*-uhlz) types of fuels made from plant materials

carbon dioxide (KAR-buhn dye-OK-side) a greenhouse gas given off when fossil fuels are burned

carbon fibers (KAR-bun FYE-burz) thin, strong strings of crystallized carbon

composite materials (kuhm-POZ-it muh-TIHR-ee-uhlz) building materials made of two or more substances combined in a way to make a strong, lightweight new product

diesel engines (DEE-zuhl EN-juhnz) a kind of internal combustion engine

emissions (ih-MISH-uhnz) substances such as gases and soot released into the air by fuel-burning engines

energy (EN-ur-jee) the power that machines such as cars and planes need in order to work

flex-fuel vehicles (FLEKS-fyoo-uhl VEE-uh-kuhlz) cars or trucks that can run on ethanol or regular gas

fluorescent lighting (fluh-RESS-uhnt LITE-ing) a kind of light made by a chemical process

fossil fuels (FOSS-uhl FYOO-uhlz) fuels such as coal, oil, and gas made from the remains of plants and animals that died millions of years ago

fuel-cell (FYOO-uhl-SEL) a device that produces electricity through a chemical reaction

global warming (GLOHB-uhl WORM-ing) the gradual heating up of Earth's air caused by greenhouse gases trapping heat from the sun in Earth's atmosphere

green (GREEN) acting in a way that is good for the environment

greenhouse gases (GREEN-*houss* GASS-iz) carbon dioxide, methane, and other gases that trap warm air in the atmosphere so it cannot escape into space; the gases responsible for global warming

hydrogen (HYE-druh-juhn) a colorless, odorless gas found in the air in large quantities

internal combustion engines (*in*-TUR-nuhl kuhm-BUSS-chuhn EN-juhnz) types of engines that run by burning fossil fuels

nonrenewable (non-re-NOO-uh-buhl) not able to be renewed or replaced by a natural process in a short period of time

oxygen (OK-suh-juhn) a colorless, odorless gas in the air that people breathe

population density (*pop*-yuh-LAY-shuhn DEN-si-tee) the total number of people living in an area per square mile

renewable (re-NOO-uh-buhl) able to be renewed or replaced by a natural process in a short period of time

sustainable (suh-STAYN-uh-buhl) a way of living that does not use up nonrenewable resources; living in a way that can be continued forever

Index

Bibliography

Hill, Graham, and Meaghan O'Neill. *Ready, Set, Green: Eight Weeks to Modern Eco-Living.* New York: Villard (2008).

McDilda, Diane Gow. *365 Ways to Live Green.* Avon, MA: Adams Media (2008).

Sperling, Daniel, and Deborah Gordon. *Two Billion Cars.* New York: Oxford University Press (2009).

Read More

Hall, Julie. *A Hot Planet Needs Cool Kids.* Bainbridge Island, WA: Green Goat Books (2007).

Murphy, Glenn. *A Kid's Guide to Global Warming.* San Francisco: Weldon Owen (2008).

Thornhill, Jan. *This Is My Planet: The Kid's Guide to Global Warming.* Toronto: Maple Tree Press (2007).

About the Author

Jacqueline A. Ball is the author of books for kids about science, nature, technology, inventions, history, and many other subjects. She lives in New York City, where she loves to walk everywhere.

WITHDRAWN